Budgeting Planner 2020
Weekly and Monthly

This Planner is Belongs To :

_____

_____

_____

_____

_____

_____

Yearly Summary

Year _____

Summary	Budget	Actual
Income		
Expense Needs		
Expense Wants		
Saving & Debt Repayment		
Total		

January

Income	
Expense Needs	
Expense Wants	
Saving & Debt Repay	
Total	

February

Income	
Expense Needs	
Expense Wants	
Saving & Debt Repay	
Total	

March

Income	
Expense Needs	
Expense Wants	
Saving & Debt Repay	
Total	

April

Income	
Expense Needs	
Expense Wants	
Saving & Debt Repay	
Total	

"Budgeting has only one rule: Do not go over budget."

-- Leslie Tayne

May

Income	
Expense Needs	
Expense Wants	
Saving & Debt Repay	
Total	

June

Income	
Expense Needs	
Expense Wants	
Saving & Debt Repay	
Total	

July

Income	
Expense Needs	
Expense Wants	
Saving & Debt Repay	
Total	

August

Income	
Expense Needs	
Expense Wants	
Saving & Debt Repay	
Total	

September

Income	
Expense Needs	
Expense Wants	
Saving & Debt Repay	
Total	

October

Income	
Expense Needs	
Expense Wants	
Saving & Debt Repay	
Total	

November

Income	
Expense Needs	
Expense Wants	
Saving & Debt Repay	
Total	

December

Income	
Expense Needs	
Expense Wants	
Saving & Debt Repay	
Total	

Account Tracker

Account No _____ *Account Balance* _____

Date	Description	Withdrawal	Deposit	Balance

Account Tracker

Account No _____ *Account Balance* _____

Date	Description	Withdrawal	Deposit	Balance

Account Tracker

Account No _____ *Account Balance* _____

Date	Description	Withdrawal	Deposit	Balance

Account Tracker

Account No _____ *Account Balance* _____

Date	Description	Withdrawal	Deposit	Balance

Saving Tracker

Savings Goal _____ *Starting Balance* _____

Date	Description	Withdrawal	Deposit	Balance

Saving Tracker

Savings Goal _____ *Starting Balance* _____

Date	Description	Withdrawal	Deposit	Balance

Saving Tracker

Savings Goal _____ *Starting Balance* _____

Date	Description	Withdrawal	Deposit	Balance

Saving Tracker

Savings Goal _____ *Starting Balance* _____

Date	Description	Withdrawal	Deposit	Balance

Debt Payment Log

*Creditor*_____

Account No.		Interest Rate	
Target Payoff Date		Credit Limit	
Account Holder		Mininum Payment	
Credit Type		Starting Balance	

Date	Payment Amount	Balance

Debt Payment Log

*Creditor*_____

Account No.		Interest Rate	
Target Payoff Date		Credit Limit	
Account Holder		Mininum Payment	
Credit Type		Starting Balance	

Date	Payment Amount	Balance

Debt Payment Log

*Creditor*_____

Account No.		Interest Rate	
Target Payoff Date		Credit Limit	
Account Holder		Mininum Payment	
Credit Type		Starting Balance	

Date	Payment Amount	Balance

Debt Payment Log

*Creditor*_____

Account No.		Interest Rate	
Target Payoff Date		Credit Limit	
Account Holder		Mininum Payment	
Credit Type		Starting Balance	

Date	Payment Amount	Balance

"Every cent you own and every moment you *spend* is always an *investment.*"

-- Natalie Pace --

January

SUN	MON	TUE	WED	THU	FRI	SAT

Monthly Budget Tracking

Monthly Income

Wages, after TAX	$
Others Income	$
Total Income	$

Expenses: Needs

Rent/Mortgage	$
Renters or homeowners	$
Insurance premiums	$
Property TAX bill	$
Auto Insurance Premiums	$
Health Insurance Premiums	$
Out-of-pocket Medical Costs	$
Life Insurance Premiums	$
Electricity & Natural gas bill	$
Water bill	$
Sanitation/Garbage bill	$
Groceries & Other Essentials	$
Car Payment	$
Parking and registration fees	$
Car maintenance & Repairs	$
Gasoline	$
Public transportion	$
Phone bill	$
Internet bill	$
Student loan payments	$
Others	$

Expense: Wants

Clothing, Jewelry, etc.	$
Dining Out	$
Special meals at home	$
Alcohol	$
Movie or event tickets	$
Gym or club memberships	$
Travel Expenses	$
Cable or streaming packages	$
Home decor items	$
Others	$

Savings and Debt Repayment

Emergency Fund Contributions	$
Savings Account Contributions	$
Individual retirement	$
Account Contributions	$
Other Investments	$
Credit Card Payments	$
Excess Payments on mortgage	$
Others	$

Monthly Budget Tracking

Budget Summary

Total Needs	$
Total Wants	$
Total Saving and Debt Repayment	$
Total Income	$
Total Spending	$
Net	$

50/30/20 Comoparison

50% for Needs	$
30% for Wants	$
20% for savings and debt repayment	$

If the 50/30/20 breakdown, recommended to adjust your spending as needed untill reach your ideal budget

Note:

_____

_____

_____

_____

_____

_____

_____

_____

_____

_____

_____

_____

_____

Daily Spending Tracking

1ˢᵗ   S   M   Tu   W   Th   F   Su

Description	Amount
Daily Total:	

2ⁿᵈ   S   M   Tu   W   Th   F   Su

Description	Amount
Daily Total:	

3ʳᵈ   S   M   Tu   W   Th   F   Su

Description	Amount
Daily Total:	

4ᵗʰ   S   M   Tu   W   Th   F   Su

Description	Amount
Daily Total:	

Daily Spending Tracking

5th S M Tu W Th F Su

Description	Amount
Daily Total:	

6th S M Tu W Th F Su

Description	Amount
Daily Total:	

7th S M Tu W Th F Su

Description	Amount
Daily Total:	

8th S M Tu W Th F Su

Description	Amount
Daily Total:	

Daily Spending Tracking

9th S M Tu W Th F Su

Description	Amount
Daily Total:	

10th S M Tu W Th F Su

Description	Amount
Daily Total:	

11st S M Tu W Th F Su

Description	Amount
Daily Total:	

12nd S M Tu W Th F Su

Description	Amount
Daily Total:	

Daily Spending Tracking

13rd S M Tu W Th F Su

Description	Amount
Daily Total:	

14th S M Tu W Th F Su

Description	Amount
Daily Total:	

15th S M Tu W Th F Su

Description	Amount
Daily Total:	

16th S M Tu W Th F Su

Description	Amount
Daily Total:	

Daily Spending Tracking

17th   S   M   Tu   W   Th   F   Su

Description	Amount
Daily Total:	

18th   S   M   Tu   W   Th   F   Su

Description	Amount
Daily Total:	

19th   S   M   Tu   W   Th   F   Su

Description	Amount
Daily Total:	

20th   S   M   Tu   W   Th   F   Su

Description	Amount
Daily Total:	

Daily Spending Tracking

21st S M Tu W Th F Su

Description	Amount
Daily Total:	

22nd S M Tu W Th F Su

Description	Amount
Daily Total:	

23rd S M Tu W Th F Su

Description	Amount
Daily Total:	

24th S M Tu W Th F Su

Description	Amount
Daily Total:	

Daily Spending Tracking

25th   S M Tu W Th F Su

Description	Amount
Daily Total:	

26th   S M Tu W Th F Su

Description	Amount
Daily Total:	

27th   S M Tu W Th F Su

Description	Amount
Daily Total:	

28th   S M Tu W Th F Su

Description	Amount
Daily Total:	

Daily Spending Tracking

29th S M Tu W Th F Su

Description	Amount
Daily Total:	

30th S M Tu W Th F Su

Description	Amount
Daily Total:	

31st S M Tu W Th F Su

Description	Amount
Daily Total:	

Monthly Budget Summary

Monthly Income	$
Total Spend	$
Net	$

Overspent ☐ ☐ ☐ ☐ ☐ Sensible

"A personal budget is
a manifestation
of your decision
to grab your finances

by the *balls*"

-- Money Tree Man --

February

SUN	MON	TUE	WED	THU	FRI	SAT

Daily Spending Tracking

1st S M Tu W Th F Su

Description	Amount
Daily Total:	

2nd S M Tu W Th F Su

Description	Amount
Daily Total:	

3rd S M Tu W Th F Su

Description	Amount
Daily Total:	

4th S M Tu W Th F Su

Description	Amount
Daily Total:	

Daily Spending Tracking

5th S M Tu W Th F Su

Description	Amount
Daily Total:	

6th S M Tu W Th F Su

Description	Amount
Daily Total:	

7th S M Tu W Th F Su

Description	Amount
Daily Total:	

8th S M Tu W Th F Su

Description	Amount
Daily Total:	

Daily Spending Tracking

9th S M Tu W Th F Su

Description	Amount
Daily Total:	

10th S M Tu W Th F Su

Description	Amount
Daily Total:	

11st S M Tu W Th F Su

Description	Amount
Daily Total:	

12nd S M Tu W Th F Su

Description	Amount
Daily Total:	

Daily Spending Tracking

13rd S M Tu W Th F Su

Description	Amount
Daily Total:	

14th S M Tu W Th F Su

Description	Amount
Daily Total:	

15th S M Tu W Th F Su

Description	Amount
Daily Total:	

16th S M Tu W Th F Su

Description	Amount
Daily Total:	

Daily Spending Tracking

17th   S   M   Tu   W   Th   F   Su

Description	Amount
Daily Total:	

18th   S   M   Tu   W   Th   F   Su

Description	Amount
Daily Total:	

19th   S   M   Tu   W   Th   F   Su

Description	Amount
Daily Total:	

20th   S   M   Tu   W   Th   F   Su

Description	Amount
Daily Total:	

Daily Spending Tracking

21st S M Tu W Th F Su

Description	Amount
Daily Total:	

22nd S M Tu W Th F Su

Description	Amount
Daily Total:	

23rd S M Tu W Th F Su

Description	Amount
Daily Total:	

24th S M Tu W Th F Su

Description	Amount
Daily Total:	

Daily Spending Tracking

25th   S   M   Tu   W   Th   F   Su

Description	Amount
Daily Total:	

26th   S   M   Tu   W   Th   F   Su

Description	Amount
Daily Total:	

27th   S   M   Tu   W   Th   F   Su

Description	Amount
Daily Total:	

28th   S   M   Tu   W   Th   F   Su

Description	Amount
Daily Total:	

Daily Spending Tracking

29*th*   S   M   Tu   W   Th   F   Su

Monthly Budget Summary

Description	Amount
Daily Total:	

Monthly Income	$
Total Spend	$
Net	$

Overspent   Sensible

Note :

Monthly Budget Tracking

Monthly Income

Wages, after TAX	$
Others Income	$
Total Income	$

Expenses: Needs

Rent/Mortgage	$
Renters or homeowners	$
Insurance premiums	$
Property TAX bill	$
Auto Insurance Premiums	$
Health Insurance Premiums	$
Out-of-pocket Medical Costs	$
Life Insurance Premiums	$
Electricity & Natural gas bill	$
Water bill	$
Sanitation/Garbage bill	$
Groceries & Other Essentials	$
Car Payment	$
Parking and registration fees	$
Car maintenance & Repairs	$
Gasoline	$
Public transportion	$
Phone bill	$
Internet bill	$
Student loan payments	$
Others	$

Expense: Wants

Clothing, Jewelry, etc.	$
Dining Out	$
Special meals at home	$
Alcohol	$
Movie or event tickets	$
Gym or club memberships	$
Travel Expenses	$
Cable or streaming packages	$
Home decor items	$
Others	$

Savings and Debt Repayment

Emergency Fund Contributions	$
Savings Account Contributions	$
Individual retirement	$
Account Contributions	$
Other Investments	$
Credit Card Payments	$
Excess Payments on mortgage	$
Others	$

Monthly Budget Tracking

Budget Summary

Total Needs	$
Total Wants	$
Total Saving and Debt Repayment	$
Total Income	$
Total Spending	$
Net	$

50/30/20 Comoparison

50% for Needs	$
30% for Wants	$
20% for savings and debt repayment	$

If the 50/30/20 breakdown, recommended to adjust your spending as needed untill reach your ideal budget

Note:

_____

_____

_____

_____

_____

_____

_____

_____

_____

_____

_____

_____

"A penny saved is worth two pennies earned . . . after taxes."

-- Randy Thurman --

March

SUN	MON	TUE	WED	THU	FRI	SAT

Monthly Budget Tracking

Monthly Income

Wages, after TAX	$
Others Income	$
Total Income	$

Expenses: Needs

Rent/Mortgage	$
Renters or homeowners	$
Insurance premiums	$
Property TAX bill	$
Auto Insurance Premiums	$
Health Insurance Premiums	$
Out-of-pocket Medical Costs	$
Life Insurance Premiums	$
Electricity & Natural gas bill	$
Water bill	$
Sanitation/Garbage bill	$
Groceries & Other Essentials	$
Car Payment	$
Parking and registration fees	$
Car maintenance & Repairs	$
Gasoline	$
Public transportion	$
Phone bill	$
Internet bill	$
Student loan payments	$
Others	$

Expense: Wants

Clothing, Jewelry, etc.	$
Dining Out	$
Special meals at home	$
Alcohol	$
Movie or event tickets	$
Gym or club memberships	$
Travel Expenses	$
Cable or streaming packages	$
Home decor items	$
Others	$

Savings and Debt Repayment

Emergency Fund Contributions	$
Savings Account Contributions	$
Individual retirement	$
Account Contributions	$
Other Investments	$
Credit Card Payments	$
Excess Payments on mortgage	$
Others	$

Monthly Budget Tracking

Budget Summary

Total Needs	$
Total Wants	$
Total Saving and Debt Repayment	$
Total Income	$
Total Spending	$
Net	$

50/30/20 Comoparison

50% for Needs	$
30% for Wants	$
20% for savings and debt repayment	$

If the 50/30/20 breakdown, recommended to adjust your spending as needed untill reach your ideal budget

Note:

Daily Spending Tracking

1st   S   M   Tu   W   Th   F   Su

Description	Amount
Daily Total:	

2nd   S   M   Tu   W   Th   F   Su

Description	Amount
Daily Total:	

3rd   S   M   Tu   W   Th   F   Su

Description	Amount
Daily Total:	

4th   S   M   Tu   W   Th   F   Su

Description	Amount
Daily Total:	

Daily Spending Tracking

5th — wait

5th S M Tu W Th F Su

Description	Amount
Daily Total:	

6th S M Tu W Th F Su

Description	Amount
Daily Total:	

7th S M Tu W Th F Su

Description	Amount
Daily Total:	

8th S M Tu W Th F Su

Description	Amount
Daily Total:	

Daily Spending Tracking

9th S M Tu W Th F Su

Description	Amount
Daily Total:	

10th S M Tu W Th F Su

Description	Amount
Daily Total:	

11st S M Tu W Th F Su

Description	Amount
Daily Total:	

12nd S M Tu W Th F Su

Description	Amount
Daily Total:	

Daily Spending Tracking

13rd S M Tu W Th F Su

Description	Amount
Daily Total:	

14th S M Tu W Th F Su

Description	Amount
Daily Total:	

15th S M Tu W Th F Su

Description	Amount
Daily Total:	

16th S M Tu W Th F Su

Description	Amount
Daily Total:	

Daily Spending Tracking

17th S M Tu W Th F Su

Description	Amount
Daily Total:	

18th S M Tu W Th F Su

Description	Amount
Daily Total:	

19th S M Tu W Th F Su

Description	Amount
Daily Total:	

20th S M Tu W Th F Su

Description	Amount
Daily Total:	

Daily Spending Tracking

21st S M Tu W Th F Su

Description	Amount
Daily Total:	

22nd S M Tu W Th F Su

Description	Amount
Daily Total:	

23rd S M Tu W Th F Su

Description	Amount
Daily Total:	

24th S M Tu W Th F Su

Description	Amount
Daily Total:	

Daily Spending Tracking

25th   S   M   Tu   W   Th   F   Su

Description	Amount
Daily Total:	

26th   S   M   Tu   W   Th   F   Su

Description	Amount
Daily Total:	

27th   S   M   Tu   W   Th   F   Su

Description	Amount
Daily Total:	

28th   S   M   Tu   W   Th   F   Su

Description	Amount
Daily Total:	

Daily Spending Tracking

29th S M Tu W Th F Su

Description	Amount
Daily Total:	

30th S M Tu W Th F Su

Description	Amount
Daily Total:	

31st S M Tu W Th F Su

Description	Amount
Daily Total:	

Monthly Budget Summary

Monthly Income	$
Total Spend	$
Net	$

Overspent   Sensible

"Don't tell me
what you value,
show me
your *budget*,
and I'll tell you
what you value."

-- Joe Biden --

April

SUN	MON	TUE	WED	THU	FRI	SAT

Monthly Budget Tracking

Monthly Income

Wages, after TAX	$
Others Income	$
Total Income	$

Expenses: Needs

Rent/Mortgage	$
Renters or homeowners	$
Insurance premiums	$
Property TAX bill	$
Auto Insurance Premiums	$
Health Insurance Premiums	$
Out-of-pocket Medical Costs	$
Life Insurance Premiums	$
Electricity & Natural gas bill	$
Water bill	$
Sanitation/Garbage bill	$
Groceries & Other Essentials	$
Car Payment	$
Parking and registration fees	$
Car maintenance & Repairs	$
Gasoline	$
Public transportion	$
Phone bill	$
Internet bill	$
Student loan payments	$
Others	$

Expense: Wants

Clothing, Jewelry, etc.	$
Dining Out	$
Special meals at home	$
Alcohol	$
Movie or event tickets	$
Gym or club memberships	$
Travel Expenses	$
Cable or streaming packages	$
Home decor items	$
Others	$

Savings and Debt Repayment

Emergency Fund Contributions	$
Savings Account Contributions	$
Individual retirement	$
Account Contributions	$
Other Investments	$
Credit Card Payments	$
Excess Payments on mortgage	$
Others	$

Monthly Budget Tracking

Budget Summary

Total Needs	$
Total Wants	$
Total Saving and Debt Repayment	$
Total Income	$
Total Spending	$
Net	$

50/30/20 Comoparison

50% for Needs	$
30% for Wants	$
20% for savings and debt repayment	$

If the 50/30/20 breakdown, recommended to adjust your spending as needed untill reach your ideal budget

Note:

Daily Spending Tracking

1st S M Tu W Th F Su

Description	Amount
Daily Total:	

2nd S M Tu W Th F Su

Description	Amount
Daily Total:	

3rd S M Tu W Th F Su

Description	Amount
Daily Total:	

4th S M Tu W Th F Su

Description	Amount
Daily Total:	

Daily Spending Tracking

5th S M Tu W Th F Su

Description	Amount
Daily Total:	

6th S M Tu W Th F Su

Description	Amount
Daily Total:	

7th S M Tu W Th F Su

Description	Amount
Daily Total:	

8th S M Tu W Th F Su

Description	Amount
Daily Total:	

Daily Spending Tracking

9th S M Tu W Th F Su

Description	Amount
Daily Total:	

10th S M Tu W Th F Su

Description	Amount
Daily Total:	

11st S M Tu W Th F Su

Description	Amount
Daily Total:	

12nd S M Tu W Th F Su

Description	Amount
Daily Total:	

Daily Spending Tracking

13rd S M Tu W Th F Su

Description	Amount
Daily Total:	

14th S M Tu W Th F Su

Description	Amount
Daily Total:	

15th S M Tu W Th F Su

Description	Amount
Daily Total:	

16th S M Tu W Th F Su

Description	Amount
Daily Total:	

Daily Spending Tracking

17th   S   M   Tu   W   Th   F   Su

Description	Amount
Daily Total:	

18th   S   M   Tu   W   Th   F   Su

Description	Amount
Daily Total:	

19th   S   M   Tu   W   Th   F   Su

Description	Amount
Daily Total:	

20th   S   M   Tu   W   Th   F   Su

Description	Amount
Daily Total:	

Daily Spending Tracking

21st S M Tu W Th F Su

Description	Amount
Daily Total:	

22nd S M Tu W Th F Su

Description	Amount
Daily Total:	

23rd S M Tu W Th F Su

Description	Amount
Daily Total:	

24th S M Tu W Th F Su

Description	Amount
Daily Total:	

Daily Spending Tracking

25th   S   M   Tu   W   Th   F   Su   **26**th   S   M   Tu   W   Th   F   Su

Description	Amount	Description	Amount
Daily Total:		Daily Total:	

27th   S   M   Tu   W   Th   F   Su   **28**th   S   M   Tu   W   Th   F   Su

Description	Amount	Description	Amount
Daily Total:		Daily Total:	

Daily Spending Tracking

29th S M Tu W Th F Su   **30th** S M Tu W Th F Su

Description	Amount	Description	Amount
Daily Total:		Daily Total:	

Note :

Monthly Budget Summary

Monthly Income	$
Total Spend	$
Net	$

Overspent   Sensible

"It isn't what you earn but how spend it that fixes your class."

-- Sinclair Lewis --

May

SUN	MON	TUE	WED	THU	FRI	SAT

Monthly Budget Tracking

Monthly Income

Wages, after TAX	$
Others Income	$
Total Income	$

Expenses: Needs

Rent/Mortgage	$
Renters or homeowners	$
Insurance premiums	$
Property TAX bill	$
Auto Insurance Premiums	$
Health Insurance Premiums	$
Out-of-pocket Medical Costs	$
Life Insurance Premiums	$
Electricity & Natural gas bill	$
Water bill	$
Sanitation/Garbage bill	$
Groceries & Other Essentials	$
Car Payment	$
Parking and registration fees	$
Car maintenance & Repairs	$
Gasoline	$
Public transportion	$
Phone bill	$
Internet bill	$
Student loan payments	$
Others	$

Expense: Wants

Clothing, Jewelry, etc.	$
Dining Out	$
Special meals at home	$
Alcohol	$
Movie or event tickets	$
Gym or club memberships	$
Travel Expenses	$
Cable or streaming packages	$
Home decor items	$
Others	$

Savings and Debt Repayment

Emergency Fund Contributions	$
Savings Account Contributions	$
Individual retirement	$
Account Contributions	$
Other Investments	$
Credit Card Payments	$
Excess Payments on mortgage	$
Others	$

Monthly Budget Tracking

Budget Summary

Total Needs	$
Total Wants	$
Total Saving and Debt Repayment	$
Total Income	$
Total Spending	$
Net	$

50/30/20 Comoparison

50% for Needs	$
30% for Wants	$
20% for savings and debt repayment	$

If the 50/30/20 breakdown, recommended to adjust your spending as needed untill reach your ideal budget

Note:

_____

_____

_____

_____

_____

_____

_____

_____

_____

_____

_____

_____

_____

_____

Daily Spending Tracking

1st   S M Tu W Th F Su

Description	Amount
Daily Total:	

2nd   S M Tu W Th F Su

Description	Amount
Daily Total:	

3rd   S M Tu W Th F Su

Description	Amount
Daily Total:	

4th   S M Tu W Th F Su

Description	Amount
Daily Total:	

Daily Spending Tracking

5th   S   M   Tu   W   Th   F   Su

Description	Amount
Daily Total:	

6th   S   M   Tu   W   Th   F   Su

Description	Amount
Daily Total:	

7th   S   M   Tu   W   Th   F   Su

Description	Amount
Daily Total:	

8th   S   M   Tu   W   Th   F   Su

Description	Amount
Daily Total:	

Daily Spending Tracking

9th S M Tu W Th F Su

Description	Amount
Daily Total:	

10th S M Tu W Th F Su

Description	Amount
Daily Total:	

11st S M Tu W Th F Su

Description	Amount
Daily Total:	

12nd S M Tu W Th F Su

Description	Amount
Daily Total:	

Daily Spending Tracking

13rd S   M   Tu   W   Th   F   Su

Description	Amount
Daily Total:	

14th S   M   Tu   W   Th   F   Su

Description	Amount
Daily Total:	

15th S   M   Tu   W   Th   F   Su

Description	Amount
Daily Total:	

16th S   M   Tu   W   Th   F   Su

Description	Amount
Daily Total:	

Daily Spending Tracking

17th   S   M   Tu   W   Th   F   Su

Description	Amount
Daily Total:	

18th   S   M   Tu   W   Th   F   Su

Description	Amount
Daily Total:	

19th   S   M   Tu   W   Th   F   Su

Description	Amount
Daily Total:	

20th   S   M   Tu   W   Th   F   Su

Description	Amount
Daily Total:	

Daily Spending Tracking

21st S M Tu W Th F Su

Description	Amount
Daily Total:	

22nd S M Tu W Th F Su

Description	Amount
Daily Total:	

23rd S M Tu W Th F Su

Description	Amount
Daily Total:	

24th S M Tu W Th F Su

Description	Amount
Daily Total:	

Daily Spending Tracking

25th   S   M   Tu   W   Th   F   Su

Description	Amount
Daily Total:	

26th   S   M   Tu   W   Th   F   Su

Description	Amount
Daily Total:	

27th   S   M   Tu   W   Th   F   Su

Description	Amount
Daily Total:	

28th   S   M   Tu   W   Th   F   Su

Description	Amount
Daily Total:	

Daily Spending Tracking

29th   S   M   Tu   W   Th   F   Su

Description	Amount
Daily Total:	

30th   S   M   Tu   W   Th   F   Su

Description	Amount
Daily Total:	

31st   S   M   Tu   W   Th   F   Su

Description	Amount
Daily Total:	

Monthly Budget Summary

Monthly Income	$
Total Spend	$
Net	$

Overspent   Sensible

"A Debt Problem
Is, At Its Core,
a Budgeting
Problem."

-- Natalie Pace --

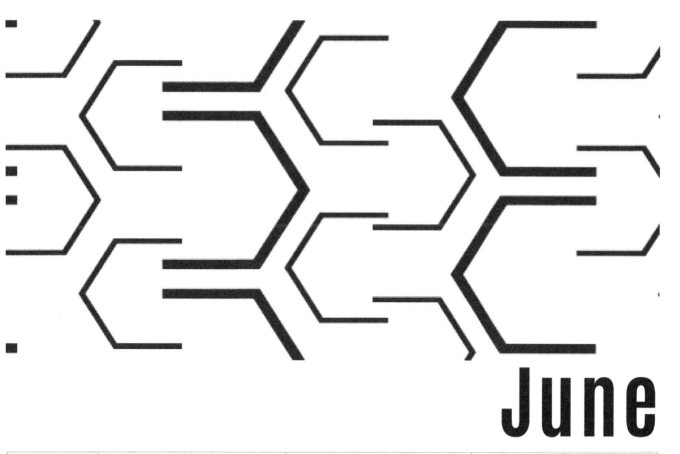

June

SUN	MON	TUE	WED	THU	FRI	SAT

Monthly Budget Tracking

Monthly Income

Wages, after TAX	$
Others Income	$
Total Income	$

Expenses: Needs

Rent/Mortgage	$
Renters or homeowners	$
Insurance premiums	$
Property TAX bill	$
Auto Insurance Premiums	$
Health Insurance Premiums	$
Out-of-pocket Medical Costs	$
Life Insurance Premiums	$
Electricity & Natural gas bill	$
Water bill	$
Sanitation/Garbage bill	$
Groceries & Other Essentials	$
Car Payment	$
Parking and registration fees	$
Car maintenance & Repairs	$
Gasoline	$
Public transportion	$
Phone bill	$
Internet bill	$
Student loan payments	$
Others	$

Expense: Wants

Clothing, Jewelry, etc.	$
Dining Out	$
Special meals at home	$
Alcohol	$
Movie or event tickets	$
Gym or club memberships	$
Travel Expenses	$
Cable or streaming packages	$
Home decor items	$
Others	$

Savings and Debt Repayment

Emergency Fund Contributions	$
Savings Account Contributions	$
Individual retirement	$
Account Contributions	$
Other Investments	$
Credit Card Payments	$
Excess Payments on mortgage	$
Others	$

Monthly Budget Tracking

Budget Summary

Total Needs	$
Total Wants	$
Total Saving and Debt Repayment	$
Total Income	$
Total Spending	$
Net	$

50/30/20 Comoparison

50% for Needs	$
30% for Wants	$
20% for savings and debt repayment	$

If the 50/30/20 breakdown, recommended to adjust your spending as needed untill reach your ideal budget

Note:

Daily Spending Tracking

1st S M Tu W Th F Su   **2nd** S M Tu W Th F Su

Description	Amount	Description	Amount
Daily Total:		Daily Total:	

3rd S M Tu W Th F Su   **4th** S M Tu W Th F Su

Description	Amount	Description	Amount
Daily Total:		Daily Total:	

Daily Spending Tracking

5th S M Tu W Th F Su

Description	Amount
Daily Total:	

6th S M Tu W Th F Su

Description	Amount
Daily Total:	

7th S M Tu W Th F Su

Description	Amount
Daily Total:	

8th S M Tu W Th F Su

Description	Amount
Daily Total:	

Daily Spending Tracking

9th   S M Tu W Th F Su

Description	Amount
Daily Total:	

10th   S M Tu W Th F Su

Description	Amount
Daily Total:	

11st   S M Tu W Th F Su

Description	Amount
Daily Total:	

12nd   S M Tu W Th F Su

Description	Amount
Daily Total:	

Daily Spending Tracking

13rd S M Tu W Th F Su

Description	Amount
Daily Total:	

14th S M Tu W Th F Su

Description	Amount
Daily Total:	

15th S M Tu W Th F Su

Description	Amount
Daily Total:	

16th S M Tu W Th F Su

Description	Amount
Daily Total:	

Daily Spending Tracking

17th S M Tu W Th F Su

Description	Amount
Daily Total:	

18th S M Tu W Th F Su

Description	Amount
Daily Total:	

19th S M Tu W Th F Su

Description	Amount
Daily Total:	

20th S M Tu W Th F Su

Description	Amount
Daily Total:	

Daily Spending Tracking

21st S M Tu W Th F Su

Description	Amount
Daily Total:	

22nd S M Tu W Th F Su

Description	Amount
Daily Total:	

23rd S M Tu W Th F Su

Description	Amount
Daily Total:	

24th S M Tu W Th F Su

Description	Amount
Daily Total:	

Daily Spending Tracking

25th   S   M   Tu   W   Th   F   Su

Description	Amount
Daily Total:	

26th   S   M   Tu   W   Th   F   Su

Description	Amount
Daily Total:	

27th   S   M   Tu   W   Th   F   Su

Description	Amount
Daily Total:	

28th   S   M   Tu   W   Th   F   Su

Description	Amount
Daily Total:	

Daily Spending Tracking

29th S   M   Tu   W   Th   F   Su

Description	Amount
Daily Total:	

30th S   M   Tu   W   Th   F   Su

Description	Amount
Daily Total:	

Note :

Monthly Budget Summary

Monthly Income	$
Total Spend	$
Net	$

Overspent   Sensible

"See money –
currency - as the flow
of energy and giving
that cycles between
you, others and me.
Now let it flow kindly,
fairly and mindfully."

-- Rasheed Ogunlaru --

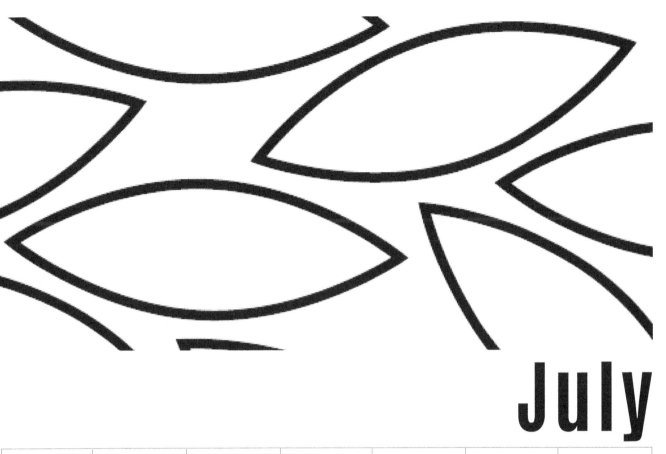

July

SUN	MON	TUE	WED	THU	FRI	SAT

Monthly Budget Tracking

Monthly Income

Wages, after TAX	$
Others Income	$
Total Income	$

Expenses: Needs

Rent/Mortgage	$
Renters or homeowners	$
Insurance premiums	$
Property TAX bill	$
Auto Insurance Premiums	$
Health Insurance Premiums	$
Out-of-pocket Medical Costs	$
Life Insurance Premiums	$
Electricity & Natural gas bill	$
Water bill	$
Sanitation/Garbage bill	$
Groceries & Other Essentials	$
Car Payment	$
Parking and registration fees	$
Car maintenance & Repairs	$
Gasoline	$
Public transportion	$
Phone bill	$
Internet bill	$
Student loan payments	$
Others	$

Expense: Wants

Clothing, Jewelry, etc.	$
Dining Out	$
Special meals at home	$
Alcohol	$
Movie or event tickets	$
Gym or club memberships	$
Travel Expenses	$
Cable or streaming packages	$
Home decor items	$
Others	$

Savings and Debt Repayment

Emergency Fund Contributions	$
Savings Account Contributions	$
Individual retirement	$
Account Contributions	$
Other Investments	$
Credit Card Payments	$
Excess Payments on mortgage	$
Others	$

Monthly Budget Tracking

Budget Summary

Total Needs	$
Total Wants	$
Total Saving and Debt Repayment	$
Total Income	$
Total Spending	$
Net	$

50/30/20 Comoparison

50% for Needs	$
30% for Wants	$
20% for savings and debt repayment	$

If the 50/30/20 breakdown, recommended to adjust your spending as needed untill reach your ideal budget

Note:

_____

_____

_____

_____

_____

_____

_____

_____

_____

_____

_____

_____

_____

_____

_____

_____

_____

Daily Spending Tracking

1st S M Tu W Th F Su   **2**nd S M Tu W Th F Su

Description	Amount
Daily Total:	

Description	Amount
Daily Total:	

3rd S M Tu W Th F Su   **4**th S M Tu W Th F Su

Description	Amount
Daily Total:	

Description	Amount
Daily Total:	

Daily Spending Tracking

5th S M Tu W Th F Su

Description	Amount
Daily Total:	

6th S M Tu W Th F Su

Description	Amount
Daily Total:	

7th S M Tu W Th F Su

Description	Amount
Daily Total:	

8th S M Tu W Th F Su

Description	Amount
Daily Total:	

Daily Spending Tracking

9th   S   M   Tu   W   Th   F   Su

Description	Amount
Daily Total:	

10th   S   M   Tu   W   Th   F   Su

Description	Amount
Daily Total:	

11st   S   M   Tu   W   Th   F   Su

Description	Amount
Daily Total:	

12nd   S   M   Tu   W   Th   F   Su

Description	Amount
Daily Total:	

Daily Spending Tracking

13rd S M Tu W Th F Su

Description	Amount
Daily Total:	

14th S M Tu W Th F Su

Description	Amount
Daily Total:	

15th S M Tu W Th F Su

Description	Amount
Daily Total:	

16th S M Tu W Th F Su

Description	Amount
Daily Total:	

Daily Spending Tracking

17th S M Tu W Th F Su   **18**th S M Tu W Th F Su

Description	Amount	Description	Amount
Daily Total:		Daily Total:	

19th S M Tu W Th F Su   **20**th S M Tu W Th F Su

Description	Amount	Description	Amount
Daily Total:		Daily Total:	

Daily Spending Tracking

21st S M Tu W Th F Su

Description	Amount
Daily Total:	

22nd S M Tu W Th F Su

Description	Amount
Daily Total:	

23rd S M Tu W Th F Su

Description	Amount
Daily Total:	

24th S M Tu W Th F Su

Description	Amount
Daily Total:	

Daily Spending Tracking

25th S M Tu W Th F Su   **26**th S M Tu W Th F Su

Description	Amount	Description	Amount
Daily Total:		Daily Total:	

27th S M Tu W Th F Su   **28**th S M Tu W Th F Su

Description	Amount	Description	Amount
Daily Total:		Daily Total:	

Daily Spending Tracking

29th S M Tu W Th F Su

Description	Amount
Daily Total:	

30th S M Tu W Th F Su

Description	Amount
Daily Total:	

31st S M Tu W Th F Su

Description	Amount
Daily Total:	

Monthly Budget Summary

Monthly Income	$
Total Spend	$
Net	$

Overspent   Sensible

"The simplest
definition of a
budget is
"telling your
money
where to go."

-- Tsh Oxenreider --

August

SUN	MON	TUE	WED	THU	FRI	SAT

Monthly Budget Tracking

Monthly Income

Wages, after TAX	$
Others Income	$
Total Income	$

Expenses: Needs

Rent/Mortgage	$
Renters or homeowners	$
Insurance premiums	$
Property TAX bill	$
Auto Insurance Premiums	$
Health Insurance Premiums	$
Out-of-pocket Medical Costs	$
Life Insurance Premiums	$
Electricity & Natural gas bill	$
Water bill	$
Sanitation/Garbage bill	$
Groceries & Other Essentials	$
Car Payment	$
Parking and registration fees	$
Car maintenance & Repairs	$
Gasoline	$
Public transportion	$
Phone bill	$
Internet bill	$
Student loan payments	$
Others	$

Expense: Wants

Clothing, Jewelry, etc.	$
Dining Out	$
Special meals at home	$
Alcohol	$
Movie or event tickets	$
Gym or club memberships	$
Travel Expenses	$
Cable or streaming packages	$
Home decor items	$
Others	$

Savings and Debt Repayment

Emergency Fund Contributions	$
Savings Account Contributions	$
Individual retirement	$
Account Contributions	$
Other Investments	$
Credit Card Payments	$
Excess Payments on mortgage	$
Others	$

Monthly Budget Tracking

Budget Summary

Total Needs	$
Total Wants	$
Total Saving and Debt Repayment	$
Total Income	$
Total Spending	$
Net	$

50/30/20 Comoparison

50% for Needs	$
30% for Wants	$
20% for savings and debt repayment	$

If the 50/30/20 breakdown, recommended to adjust your spending as needed untill reach your ideal budget

Note:

Daily Spending Tracking

1st   S M Tu W Th F Su

Description	Amount
Daily Total:	

2nd   S M Tu W Th F Su

Description	Amount
Daily Total:	

3rd   S M Tu W Th F Su

Description	Amount
Daily Total:	

4th   S M Tu W Th F Su

Description	Amount
Daily Total:	

Daily Spending Tracking

5th S M Tu W Th F Su

Description	Amount
Daily Total:	

6th S M Tu W Th F Su

Description	Amount
Daily Total:	

7th S M Tu W Th F Su

Description	Amount
Daily Total:	

8th S M Tu W Th F Su

Description	Amount
Daily Total:	

Daily Spending Tracking

9th   S   M   Tu   W   Th   F   Su   **10th**   S   M   Tu   W   Th   F   Su

Description	Amount	Description	Amount
Daily Total:		Daily Total:	

11st   S   M   Tu   W   Th   F   Su   **12nd**   S   M   Tu   W   Th   F   Su

Description	Amount	Description	Amount
Daily Total:		Daily Total:	

Daily Spending Tracking

13rd S M Tu W Th F Su

Description	Amount
Daily Total:	

14th S M Tu W Th F Su

Description	Amount
Daily Total:	

15th S M Tu W Th F Su

Description	Amount
Daily Total:	

16th S M Tu W Th F Su

Description	Amount
Daily Total:	

Daily Spending Tracking

17th   S M Tu W Th F Su   **18**th   S M Tu W Th F Su

Description	Amount
Daily Total:	

Description	Amount
Daily Total:	

19th   S M Tu W Th F Su   **20**th   S M Tu W Th F Su

Description	Amount
Daily Total:	

Description	Amount
Daily Total:	

Daily Spending Tracking

21st S M Tu W Th F Su

Description	Amount
Daily Total:	

22nd S M Tu W Th F Su

Description	Amount
Daily Total:	

23rd S M Tu W Th F Su

Description	Amount
Daily Total:	

24th S M Tu W Th F Su

Description	Amount
Daily Total:	

Daily Spending Tracking

25th   S   M   Tu   W   Th   F   Su

Description	Amount
Daily Total:	

26th   S   M   Tu   W   Th   F   Su

Description	Amount
Daily Total:	

27th   S   M   Tu   W   Th   F   Su

Description	Amount
Daily Total:	

28th   S   M   Tu   W   Th   F   Su

Description	Amount
Daily Total:	

Daily Spending Tracking

29th S M Tu W Th F Su

Description	Amount
Daily Total:	

30th S M Tu W Th F Su

Description	Amount
Daily Total:	

31st S M Tu W Th F Su

Description	Amount
Daily Total:	

Monthly Budget Summary

Monthly Income	$
Total Spend	$
Net	$

Overspent   Sensible

"A budget tells us what we can't afford, but it doesn't keep us from buying it."

-- William Feather --

September

SUN	MON	TUE	WED	THU	FRI	SAT

Monthly Budget Tracking

Monthly Income

Wages, after TAX	$
Others Income	$
Total Income	$

Expenses: Needs

Rent/Mortgage	$
Renters or homeowners	$
Insurance premiums	$
Property TAX bill	$
Auto Insurance Premiums	$
Health Insurance Premiums	$
Out-of-pocket Medical Costs	$
Life Insurance Premiums	$
Electricity & Natural gas bill	$
Water bill	$
Sanitation/Garbage bill	$
Groceries & Other Essentials	$
Car Payment	$
Parking and registration fees	$
Car maintenance & Repairs	$
Gasoline	$
Public transportion	$
Phone bill	$
Internet bill	$
Student loan payments	$
Others	$

Expense: Wants

Clothing, Jewelry, etc.	$
Dining Out	$
Special meals at home	$
Alcohol	$
Movie or event tickets	$
Gym or club memberships	$
Travel Expenses	$
Cable or streaming packages	$
Home decor items	$
Others	$

Savings and Debt Repayment

Emergency Fund Contributions	$
Savings Account Contributions	$
Individual retirement	$
Account Contributions	$
Other Investments	$
Credit Card Payments	$
Excess Payments on mortgage	$
Others	$

Monthly Budget Tracking

Budget Summary

Total Needs	$
Total Wants	$
Total Saving and Debt Repayment	$
Total Income	$
Total Spending	$
Net	$

50/30/20 Comoparison

50% for Needs	$
30% for Wants	$
20% for savings and debt repayment	$

If the 50/30/20 breakdown, recommended to adjust your spending as needed untill reach your ideal budget

Note:

Daily Spending Tracking

1st — use the form below

1st S M Tu W Th F Su

Description	Amount
Daily Total:	

2nd S M Tu W Th F Su

Description	Amount
Daily Total:	

3rd S M Tu W Th F Su

Description	Amount
Daily Total:	

4th S M Tu W Th F Su

Description	Amount
Daily Total:	

Daily Spending Tracking

5th S M Tu W Th F Su

Description	Amount
Daily Total:	

6th S M Tu W Th F Su

Description	Amount
Daily Total:	

7th S M Tu W Th F Su

Description	Amount
Daily Total:	

8th S M Tu W Th F Su

Description	Amount
Daily Total:	

Daily Spending Tracking

9th S M Tu W Th F Su

Description	Amount
Daily Total:	

10th S M Tu W Th F Su

Description	Amount
Daily Total:	

11st S M Tu W Th F Su

Description	Amount
Daily Total:	

12nd S M Tu W Th F Su

Description	Amount
Daily Total:	

Daily Spending Tracking

13rd S M Tu W Th F Su

Description	Amount
Daily Total:	

14th S M Tu W Th F Su

Description	Amount
Daily Total:	

15th S M Tu W Th F Su

Description	Amount
Daily Total:	

16th S M Tu W Th F Su

Description	Amount
Daily Total:	

Daily Spending Tracking

17th S M Tu W Th F Su   **18**th S M Tu W Th F Su

Description	Amount
Daily Total:	

Description	Amount
Daily Total:	

19th S M Tu W Th F Su   **20**th S M Tu W Th F Su

Description	Amount
Daily Total:	

Description	Amount
Daily Total:	

Daily Spending Tracking

21st S M Tu W Th F Su

Description	Amount
Daily Total:	

22nd S M Tu W Th F Su

Description	Amount
Daily Total:	

23rd S M Tu W Th F Su

Description	Amount
Daily Total:	

24th S M Tu W Th F Su

Description	Amount
Daily Total:	

Daily Spending Tracking

25th   S   M   Tu   W   Th   F   Su

Description	Amount
Daily Total:	

26th   S   M   Tu   W   Th   F   Su

Description	Amount
Daily Total:	

27th   S   M   Tu   W   Th   F   Su

Description	Amount
Daily Total:	

28th   S   M   Tu   W   Th   F   Su

Description	Amount
Daily Total:	

Daily Spending Tracking

29th S M Tu W Th F Su

Description	Amount
Daily Total:	

30th S M Tu W Th F Su

Description	Amount
Daily Total:	

Note :

Monthly Budget Summary

Monthly Income	$
Total Spend	$
Net	$

Overspent   Sensible

"Budgeting is not just for people who do not have enough money. It is for everyone who wants to ensure that their money is enough."

-- Rosette Mugidde Wamambe --

October

SUN	MON	TUE	WED	THU	FRI	SAT

Monthly Budget Tracking

Monthly Income

Wages, after TAX	$
Others Income	$
Total Income	$

Expenses: Needs

Rent/Mortgage	$
Renters or homeowners	$
Insurance premiums	$
Property TAX bill	$
Auto Insurance Premiums	$
Health Insurance Premiums	$
Out-of-pocket Medical Costs	$
Life Insurance Premiums	$
Electricity & Natural gas bill	$
Water bill	$
Sanitation/Garbage bill	$
Groceries & Other Essentials	$
Car Payment	$
Parking and registration fees	$
Car maintenance & Repairs	$
Gasoline	$
Public transportion	$
Phone bill	$
Internet bill	$
Student loan payments	$
Others	$

Expense: Wants

Clothing, Jewelry, etc.	$
Dining Out	$
Special meals at home	$
Alcohol	$
Movie or event tickets	$
Gym or club memberships	$
Travel Expenses	$
Cable or streaming packages	$
Home decor items	$
Others	$

Savings and Debt Repayment

Emergency Fund Contributions	$
Savings Account Contributions	$
Individual retirement	$
Account Contributions	$
Other Investments	$
Credit Card Payments	$
Excess Payments on mortgage	$
Others	$

Monthly Budget Tracking

Budget Summary

Total Needs	$
Total Wants	$
Total Saving and Debt Repayment	$
Total Income	$
Total Spending	$
Net	$

50/30/20 Comoparison

50% for Needs	$
30% for Wants	$
20% for savings and debt repayment	$

If the 50/30/20 breakdown, recommended to adjust your spending as needed untill reach your ideal budget

Note:

Daily Spending Tracking

1st   S   M   Tu   W   Th   F   Su   **2nd**   S   M   Tu   W   Th   F   Su

Description	Amount	Description	Amount
Daily Total:		Daily Total:	

3rd   S   M   Tu   W   Th   F   Su   **4th**   S   M   Tu   W   Th   F   Su

Description	Amount	Description	Amount
Daily Total:		Daily Total:	

Daily Spending Tracking

5th S M Tu W Th F Su

Description	Amount
Daily Total:	

6th S M Tu W Th F Su

Description	Amount
Daily Total:	

7th S M Tu W Th F Su

Description	Amount
Daily Total:	

8th S M Tu W Th F Su

Description	Amount
Daily Total:	

Daily Spending Tracking

9th   S   M   Tu   W   Th   F   Su

Description	Amount
Daily Total:	

10th   S   M   Tu   W   Th   F   Su

Description	Amount
Daily Total:	

11st   S   M   Tu   W   Th   F   Su

Description	Amount
Daily Total:	

12nd   S   M   Tu   W   Th   F   Su

Description	Amount
Daily Total:	

Daily Spending Tracking

13rd   S   M   Tu   W   Th   F   Su

Description	Amount
Daily Total:	

14th   S   M   Tu   W   Th   F   Su

Description	Amount
Daily Total:	

15th   S   M   Tu   W   Th   F   Su

Description	Amount
Daily Total:	

16th   S   M   Tu   W   Th   F   Su

Description	Amount
Daily Total:	

Daily Spending Tracking

17th   S   M   Tu   W   Th   F   Su

Description	Amount
Daily Total:	

18th   S   M   Tu   W   Th   F   Su

Description	Amount
Daily Total:	

19th   S   M   Tu   W   Th   F   Su

Description	Amount
Daily Total:	

20th   S   M   Tu   W   Th   F   Su

Description	Amount
Daily Total:	

Daily Spending Tracking

21ˢᵗ S M Tu W Th F Su

Description	Amount
Daily Total:	

22ⁿᵈ S M Tu W Th F Su

Description	Amount
Daily Total:	

23ʳᵈ S M Tu W Th F Su

Description	Amount
Daily Total:	

24ᵗʰ S M Tu W Th F Su

Description	Amount
Daily Total:	

Daily Spending Tracking

25th   S   M   Tu   W   Th   F   Su

Description	Amount
Daily Total:	

26th   S   M   Tu   W   Th   F   Su

Description	Amount
Daily Total:	

27th   S   M   Tu   W   Th   F   Su

Description	Amount
Daily Total:	

28th   S   M   Tu   W   Th   F   Su

Description	Amount
Daily Total:	

Daily Spending Tracking

29th   S   M   Tu   W   Th   F   Su

Description	Amount
Daily Total:	

30th   S   M   Tu   W   Th   F   Su

Description	Amount
Daily Total:	

31st   S   M   Tu   W   Th   F   Su

Description	Amount
Daily Total:	

Monthly Budget Summary

Monthly Income	$
Total Spend	$
Net	$

Overspent   Sensible

"A 3% budget increase is a timid goal in a business environment where timidity/ irresoluteness loses"

-- Fritz Shoemaker --

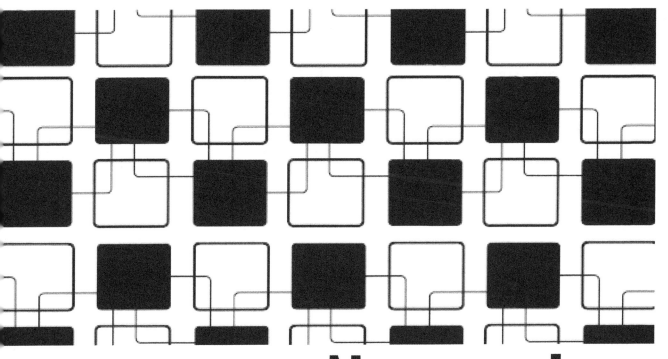

November

SUN	MON	TUE	WED	THU	FRI	SAT

Monthly Budget Tracking

Monthly Income

Wages, after TAX	$
Others Income	$
Total Income	$

Expenses: Needs

Rent/Mortgage	$
Renters or homeowners	$
Insurance premiums	$
Property TAX bill	$
Auto Insurance Premiums	$
Health Insurance Premiums	$
Out-of-pocket Medical Costs	$
Life Insurance Premiums	$
Electricity & Natural gas bill	$
Water bill	$
Sanitation/Garbage bill	$
Groceries & Other Essentials	$
Car Payment	$
Parking and registration fees	$
Car maintenance & Repairs	$
Gasoline	$
Public transportion	$
Phone bill	$
Internet bill	$
Student loan payments	$
Others	$

Expense: Wants

Clothing, Jewelry, etc.	$
Dining Out	$
Special meals at home	$
Alcohol	$
Movie or event tickets	$
Gym or club memberships	$
Travel Expenses	$
Cable or streaming packages	$
Home decor items	$
Others	$

Savings and Debt Repayment

Emergency Fund Contributions	$
Savings Account Contributions	$
Individual retirement	$
Account Contributions	$
Other Investments	$
Credit Card Payments	$
Excess Payments on mortgage	$
Others	$

Monthly Budget Tracking

Budget Summary

Total Needs	$
Total Wants	$
Total Saving and Debt Repayment	$
Total Income	$
Total Spending	$
Net	$

50/30/20 Comoparison

50% for Needs	$
30% for Wants	$
20% for savings and debt repayment	$

If the 50/30/20 breakdown, recommended to adjust your spending as needed untill reach your ideal budget

Note:

_____

_____

_____

_____

_____

_____

_____

_____

_____

_____

_____

_____

Daily Spending Tracking

1st S M Tu W Th F Su   **2nd** S M Tu W Th F Su

Description	Amount		Description	Amount
Daily Total:			Daily Total:	

3rd S M Tu W Th F Su   **4th** S M Tu W Th F Su

Description	Amount		Description	Amount
Daily Total:			Daily Total:	

Daily Spending Tracking

5th S M Tu W Th F Su

Description	Amount
Daily Total:	

6th S M Tu W Th F Su

Description	Amount
Daily Total:	

7th S M Tu W Th F Su

Description	Amount
Daily Total:	

8th S M Tu W Th F Su

Description	Amount
Daily Total:	

Daily Spending Tracking

9th   S   M   Tu   W   Th   F   Su

Description	Amount
Daily Total:	

10th   S   M   Tu   W   Th   F   Su

Description	Amount
Daily Total:	

11st   S   M   Tu   W   Th   F   Su

Description	Amount
Daily Total:	

12nd   S   M   Tu   W   Th   F   Su

Description	Amount
Daily Total:	

Daily Spending Tracking

13rd S M Tu W Th F Su

Description	Amount
Daily Total:	

14th S M Tu W Th F Su

Description	Amount
Daily Total:	

15th S M Tu W Th F Su

Description	Amount
Daily Total:	

16th S M Tu W Th F Su

Description	Amount
Daily Total:	

Daily Spending Tracking

17th S M Tu W Th F Su   **18**th S M Tu W Th F Su

Description	Amount
Daily Total:	

Description	Amount
Daily Total:	

19th S M Tu W Th F Su   **20**th S M Tu W Th F Su

Description	Amount
Daily Total:	

Description	Amount
Daily Total:	

Daily Spending Tracking

21st S M Tu W Th F Su

Description	Amount
Daily Total:	

22nd S M Tu W Th F Su

Description	Amount
Daily Total:	

23rd S M Tu W Th F Su

Description	Amount
Daily Total:	

24th S M Tu W Th F Su

Description	Amount
Daily Total:	

Daily Spending Tracking

25th S M Tu W Th F Su

Description	Amount
Daily Total:	

26th S M Tu W Th F Su

Description	Amount
Daily Total:	

27th S M Tu W Th F Su

Description	Amount
Daily Total:	

28th S M Tu W Th F Su

Description	Amount
Daily Total:	

Daily Spending Tracking

29th S M Tu W Th F Su   30th S M Tu W Th F Su

Description	Amount	Description	Amount
Daily Total:		Daily Total:	

Note :

Monthly Budget Summary

Monthly Income	$
Total Spend	$
Net	$

Overspent   Sensible

"Too many people
spend money
they haven't earned,
to buy things
they don't want,
to impress people
that they don't like."

-- Will Rogers --

December

SUN	MON	TUE	WED	THU	FRI	SAT

Monthly Budget Tracking

Monthly Income

Wages, after TAX	$
Others Income	$
Total Income	$

Expenses: Needs

Rent/Mortgage	$
Renters or homeowners	$
Insurance premiums	$
Property TAX bill	$
Auto Insurance Premiums	$
Health Insurance Premiums	$
Out-of-pocket Medical Costs	$
Life Insurance Premiums	$
Electricity & Natural gas bill	$
Water bill	$
Sanitation/Garbage bill	$
Groceries & Other Essentials	$
Car Payment	$
Parking and registration fees	$
Car maintenance & Repairs	$
Gasoline	$
Public transportion	$
Phone bill	$
Internet bill	$
Student loan payments	$
Others	$

Expense: Wants

Clothing, Jewelry, etc.	$
Dining Out	$
Special meals at home	$
Alcohol	$
Movie or event tickets	$
Gym or club memberships	$
Travel Expenses	$
Cable or streaming packages	$
Home decor items	$
Others	$

Savings and Debt Repayment

Emergency Fund Contributions	$
Savings Account Contributions	$
Individual retirement	$
Account Contributions	$
Other Investments	$
Credit Card Payments	$
Excess Payments on mortgage	$
Others	$

Monthly Budget Tracking

Budget Summary

Total Needs	$
Total Wants	$
Total Saving and Debt Repayment	$
Total Income	$
Total Spending	$
Net	$

50/30/20 Comoparison

50% for Needs	$
30% for Wants	$
20% for savings and debt repayment	$

If the 50/30/20 breakdown, recommended to adjust
your spending as needed untill reach your ideal budget

Note:

_____

_____

_____

_____

_____

_____

_____

_____

_____

_____

_____

_____

_____

Daily Spending Tracking

1st S M Tu W Th F Su

Description	Amount
Daily Total:	

2nd S M Tu W Th F Su

Description	Amount
Daily Total:	

3rd S M Tu W Th F Su

Description	Amount
Daily Total:	

4th S M Tu W Th F Su

Description	Amount
Daily Total:	

Daily Spending Tracking

5th S M Tu W Th F Su

Description	Amount
Daily Total:	

6th S M Tu W Th F Su

Description	Amount
Daily Total:	

7th S M Tu W Th F Su

Description	Amount
Daily Total:	

8th S M Tu W Th F Su

Description	Amount
Daily Total:	

Daily Spending Tracking

9th   S   M   Tu   W   Th   F   Su

Description	Amount
Daily Total:	

10th   S   M   Tu   W   Th   F   Su

Description	Amount
Daily Total:	

11st   S   M   Tu   W   Th   F   Su

Description	Amount
Daily Total:	

12nd   S   M   Tu   W   Th   F   Su

Description	Amount
Daily Total:	

Daily Spending Tracking

13rd S M Tu W Th F Su

Description	Amount
Daily Total:	

14th S M Tu W Th F Su

Description	Amount
Daily Total:	

15th S M Tu W Th F Su

Description	Amount
Daily Total:	

16th S M Tu W Th F Su

Description	Amount
Daily Total:	

Daily Spending Tracking

17th S M Tu W Th F Su   18th S M Tu W Th F Su

Description	Amount	Description	Amount
Daily Total:		Daily Total:	

19th S M Tu W Th F Su   20th S M Tu W Th F Su

Description	Amount	Description	Amount
Daily Total:		Daily Total:	

Daily Spending Tracking

21st S M Tu W Th F Su

Description	Amount
Daily Total:	

22nd S M Tu W Th F Su

Description	Amount
Daily Total:	

23rd S M Tu W Th F Su

Description	Amount
Daily Total:	

24th S M Tu W Th F Su

Description	Amount
Daily Total:	

Daily Spending Tracking

25ᵗʰ S M Tu W Th F Su   **26ᵗʰ** S M Tu W Th F Su

Description	Amount
Daily Total:	

Description	Amount
Daily Total:	

27ᵗʰ S M Tu W Th F Su   **28ᵗʰ** S M Tu W Th F Su

Description	Amount
Daily Total:	

Description	Amount
Daily Total:	

Daily Spending Tracking

29th S M Tu W Th F Su

Description	Amount
Daily Total:	

30th S M Tu W Th F Su

Description	Amount
Daily Total:	

31st S M Tu W Th F Su

Description	Amount
Daily Total:	

Monthly Budget Summary

Monthly Income	$
Total Spend	$
Net	$

Overspent ☐ ☐ ☐ ☐ ☐ Sensible

Made in the USA
Coppell, TX
05 July 2024

34294480R10092